United States Air Force

Irregular Warfare Strategy

2013

**To Organize, Train, and Equip
To Achieve Strategic Guidance**

FOREWORD

We are pleased to provide the United States Air Force Irregular Warfare (IW) Strategy to guide how our Service will meet recent national strategic direction concerning IW.

To date, America's IW operations and activities have often reacted to crises affecting American strategic interests directly or through challenges to key partner nations. However, the latest strategic level guidance from the President of the United States, Secretary of Defense and the Chairman of the Joint Chiefs of Staff requires a shift from crisis reaction to more deliberate, long-term IW activities coordinated with all "3D" (diplomacy, development, and defense) whole-of-government approaches intended to shape the global security environment and prevent conflict. Peacetime engagement to shape strategic conditions is now a key focus of American strategy.

Air, space and cyberspace power are among the most powerful tools in shaping a safe and stable world to achieve U.S. strategic objectives. Their value is already well-known in the context of conventional warfare and direct action IW. Planned and properly resourced air, space and cyberspace capabilities can also play a vital role in proactively shaping the global environment and addressing irregular challenges through indirect, cost-effective means such as security cooperation by, with and through partner nations.

The Air Force cannot treat irregular warfare as a temporary mission it can accommodate with mismatched conventional forces. Neither can the Air Force lean entirely on special operations forces to carry the IW mission. IW has become a mainstream mission. The human capital required to conduct IW is embedded throughout the Total Force. We will effectively and efficiently take advantage of that capital. Advising and training partner nations shall be part of the fundamental identity, culture and expectation of Airmen. We will develop Airmen able to build and maintain regional, cultural, and language expertise, demonstrate air advising skills, and think strategically about how peacetime engagement operations can shape geopolitical relationships to support enduring U.S. strategic interests.

In strategist B.H. Liddell Hart's words, the true aim of strategy "is not so much to seek battle, as to seek a strategic situation so advantageous that if it does not of itself produce the decision, its continuation by a battle is sure to."[1] Effective IW capabilities are critical tools for the United States to achieve this aim.

Eric K. Fanning
Acting Secretary of the Air Force

MARK A. WELSH III
General, USAF
Chief of Staff

---

[1] B.H. Liddell Hart, *Strategy: the Indirect Approach* (London: Faber & Faber Ltd., 1941), 339.

"Building [partner] capacity elsewhere in the world also remains important for sharing the cost and responsibilities of global leadership. Across the globe we will seek to be the security partner of choice, pursuing new partnerships with a growing number of nations – including those in Africa and Latin America – whose interests and viewpoints are merging into a common vision of freedom, stability, and prosperity. **Whenever possible, we will develop innovative, low-cost, and small-footprint approaches to achieve our security objectives**, *relying on exercises, rotational presence, and advisory capabilities…*

U.S. forces will conduct a sustainable pace of presence operations abroad, including rotational deployments and bilateral and multilateral training exercises. These activities reinforce deterrence, help to build the capacity and competence of U.S., allied, and partner forces for internal and external defense, strengthen alliance cohesion, and increase U.S. influence. A reduction in resources will require innovative and creative solutions to maintain our support for allied and partner interoperability and building partner capacity. **However, with reduced resources, thoughtful choices will need to be made regarding the location and frequency of these operations."**

– Sustaining U.S. Global Leadership: Priorities for 21st Century Defense, January 2012, Secretary of Defense (original emphasis), 3, 5-6.

EXECUTIVE SUMMARY

This updated United States Air Force (USAF) Irregular Warfare (IW) Strategy provides direction for the USAF to organize, train, and equip to provide capabilities necessary to meet strategic guidance related to IW. Since the USAF published its initial IW Strategy in 2009, national strategic guidance has sought to rebalance IW:

- From large-scale operations to low-cost, small footprint approaches;

- From direct U.S. operations to indirect actions by, with, and through partner nations;

- From large-scale counterinsurgency and stability operations in Iraq and Afghanistan to a more distributed, though carefully prioritized, global effort focusing more on the Asia-Pacific region;

- From crisis response, near-term focused efforts to more deliberate, long-term efforts closely tied to enduring U.S. strategic interests; and

- From predominantly a special operations force mission to one institutionalized across the general purpose force.

In addition, recent studies have identified shortfalls and challenges that negatively impact the USAF's ability to execute this strategic guidance concerning IW (see Appendix D for details). They include: the lack of a coordinated U.S. government strategy and execution; authorities that do not support long-term planning and execution timelines; capability and manpower shortfalls; the lack of "right tech" USAF platforms to transfer to partner nations; limited funding; and inadequate IW education and training.

Therefore, to address this updated strategic guidance given these challenges, the USAF IW Strategy to organize, train, and equip is to:

1. Adopt a partnering culture;
2. Influence U.S. global shaping activities guided by a new USAF Aviation Enterprise Development Vision and Strategy;
3. Advocate IW authorities that enable effective, long-term, persistent engagements;
4. Establish the means to meet global light aviation demands with American aircraft and services;
5. Adequately man planning staffs associated with IW;
6. Excel at IW-related planning, resourcing, execution, and assessment;
7. Develop a USAF concept and strategy using general purpose forces to support unconventional warfare;
8. Address USAF shortfalls in conducting direct IW operations; and
9. Implement the *USAF IW Operations Roadmap FY12-FY16*.

"In identifying [centers of gravity], it is important to remember that irregular warfare focuses on legitimacy and influence over a population, unlike traditional warfare, which employs direct military confrontation to defeat an adversary's armed forces, destroys an adversary's war-making capacity, or seizes or retains territory to force a change in an adversary's government or policies."

- Joint Publication 5-0, *Joint Operation Planning*, III-22.

1. PURPOSE

This updated United States Air Force (USAF) Irregular Warfare (IW) Strategy provides direction for the USAF to organize, train, and equip to provide capabilities necessary to meet strategic guidance related to IW.[2] In doing so, this document also makes the case to Airmen as to why effectively conducting IW is not only important to achieve United States (U.S.) national security objectives, but also to enhance the USAF's abilities to effectively operate in the air, space, and cyberspace domains for the foreseeable future.

In January 2009, the USAF published *The 21st Century Air Force Irregular Warfare Strategy*, a white paper to "provide definitive guidance to initiate new approaches and synchronize Air Force actions to balance the requirements levied upon airpower in irregular warfare with the concurrent need to maintain decisive advantage in conventional warfare" and "chart a strategy to adapt to the irregular challenges of the 21st Century."[3] It described the nature of IW challenges, the role of airpower in the IW environment, the need to become proficient in IW, and seven initiatives towards that end.

Since its publication, the USAF has made progress in institutionalizing IW and enhancing its IW capabilities to help achieve U.S. national security objectives (see Appendix A for details). However, also during this period:

- Strategic guidance from the President of the United States, the Office of the Secretary of Defense (OSD), and the Chairman of the Joint Chiefs of Staff (CJCS) relevant to IW has been expanded, refined, and updated.

- Several studies by the Joint Staff and the USAF have highlighted critical shortfalls and challenges affecting USAF conduct of IW that need to be fixed to address this strategic guidance.

---

[2] "Strategy" in the context of this document is not a "set of ideas for employing the instruments of national power in a synchronized and integrated fashion to achieve theater, national, and/or multinational objectives" as defined by the Department of Defense (DOD), but rather strategy in the more general sense of a flexible, adaptable blueprint to accomplish a specific goal (in this case, organizing, training, and equipping to execute strategic guidance concerning IW).

[3] U.S. Air Force, *The 21st Century Air Force Irregular Warfare Strategy*, January 2009, 3.

- USAF IW doctrine has been updated and effectively covers much of the content of the 2009 USAF IW Strategy.

This document replaces the initial USAF IW Strategy in order to update its content to remain consistent with the developments above. It first provides the context underlying this strategy by briefly summarizing: (1) what IW is; (2) how airpower (which includes air, space, and cyberspace power) contributes to IW-related operations and activities; (3) the changes in strategic guidance related to IW relevant to the USAF; and (4) documented shortfalls and challenges facing USAF IW operations before describing the USAF's IW strategy to address the new guidance and challenges. All other ongoing USAF efforts to organize, train, and equip to conduct IW not affected by the initiatives of this USAF IW Strategy should continue as before, subject to all relevant policy and guidance (largely compiled in Appendix B).

Several of the initiatives in this USAF IW Strategy will require a relatively small amount of additional funding and/or manpower (or at least maintaining current funding and/or manpower). It is not the purpose of this document to identify trade space to fund the IW needs it highlights. The USAF Corporate Structure makes such decisions during the development and review of the Program Objective Memorandum (POM), which reflects strategic guidance as best as possible given fiscal constraints.

2. STRATEGIC CONTEXT

What is IW?

Irregular warfare is defined and scoped in detail in various Department of Defense (DOD) policy, doctrine, and concept publications (listed in Appendix B). While this document will not restate every detail here, it will summarize key concepts and guiding principles to provide useful context and logic flow for both the strategic guidance on IW and this USAF IW Strategy.

DOD defines IW as a "violent struggle among state and non-state actors for legitimacy and influence over the relevant populations. IW favors indirect and asymmetric approaches, though it may employ the full range of military and other capabilities in order to erode an adversary's power, influence and will."[4] According to the consensus of the intelligence and military communities summarized in the *USAF Strategic Environmental Assessment, 2010-2030*, the rise of IW-related challenges has been driven by various trends and developments that are expected to continue for at least the next twenty years (summarized in Appendix C).

---

[4] U.S. Department of Defense, Joint Publication 1-02: *Dictionary of Military and Associated Terms*, 148.

According to the most recent IW Joint Operating Concept (JOC), the **IW problem is that adaptive adversaries, such as terrorists, insurgents, and transnational criminal networks, present irregular threats to U.S. partner nations (PNs)[5] that are not readily countered by traditional military means alone.**[6] These threats:

- Compete with PNs for legitimacy and influence over relevant populations;

- Are enmeshed in the population of PNs;

- Extend their reach and impact regionally and globally through use of communications, cyberspace, technology, and personal relationships fostered by providing services in underserved areas; and

- Require long-term efforts to address.

The IW JOC also highlights that irregular threats present additional challenges that compound the IW problem for the joint force:

- Complex political, cultural, religious, and historic factors, as well as the diverse populations involved in each irregular conflict, are difficult to understand in sufficient depth.

- The use of direct military force can backfire by rallying opposition.

- The non-military nature of many aspects of these conflicts fall outside the sole competence of the joint force.

- Many irregular actors are proficient in waging the battle of the narrative.

- The protracted nature of IW tests U.S. staying power.

- U.S. PNs often cannot meet the needs of their society, which in turn affects their political legitimacy and strengthens the appeal of internal irregular threats. These needs are often filled instead by those irregular threats.

- Irregular threats often use cyberspace for safe havens, recruiting, and means of attack.

- IW threats often operate as networks outside the governing bodies of the country.

- IW threats are often decentralized.

---

[5] "Partner nations" and "host nations" are used almost interchangeably by IW-related guidance and doctrine. While they are almost always the same, DOD defines a partner nation as "a nation that the United States works with in a specific situation or operation." U.S. Department of Defense, Joint Publication 1: *Doctrine for the Armed Forces of the United States*, March 25, 2013, GL-10. DOD defines a host nation as "a nation which receives the forces and/or supplies of allied nations and/or [North American Treaty Organization] organizations to be located on, to operate in, or to transit through its territory." U.S. Department of Defense, Joint Publication 3-57: *Civil-Military Operations*, July 8, 2008, GL-9. This document prefers to use the broader term "partner nations."

[6] U.S. Department of Defense, Chairman of the Joint Chiefs of Staff, *Irregular Warfare: Countering Irregular Threats Joint Operating Concept, Version 2.0*, May 17, 2010, 14-15.

The IW JOC emphasizes **"the contest for legitimacy and influence over a population will be won primarily through persistent effort to enable a legitimate and capable local partner to address the conflict's causes and provide security, good governance, and economic development."**[7] U.S. government efforts to assist PNs to prevail in this contest primarily consist of security sector assistance (SSA),[8] which is led and coordinated by the Department of State and governed by Presidential Policy Directive/PPD-23, *Security Sector Assistance*. The Departments of Defense, Treasury, Justice, Transportation, and Homeland Security, as well as the U.S. Agency for International Development, also play major roles in SSA.

DOD's primary way of supporting SSA is to provide security cooperation[9] (SC) assistance aimed at building partner capacity.[10] These efforts are designed to help a PN eventually become self-sufficient and take care of its own challenges with its own resources. As described in the *2011 USAF Global Partnership Strategy* and the *USAF Air Advising Operating Concept*, **the USAF piece of the DOD's SC effort is to help develop, enhance, and sustain a PN's aviation enterprise to meet its needs and desires and to deliver a level of access and capability that supports U.S. strategic objectives.**[11] USAF IW doctrine notes "enhanced aviation enterprise capabilities enable [PNs] to strengthen internal security, defend against external aggression, and act as trusted participants in regional security structures. [PNs] can then help prevent festering problems from turning into crises that may require costly U.S. intervention."[12]

---

[7] U.S. Department of Defense, Chairman of the Joint Chiefs of Staff, *Irregular Warfare: Countering Irregular Threats Joint Operating Concept, Version 2.0*, May 17, 2010, 16-17. USAF IW doctrine similarly notes that "the desired IW end state is a self-sufficient partner with a supportive population." Air Force Doctrine Document 3-2: *Irregular Warfare,* March 15, 2013, 12

[8] SSA refers to "the policies, programs, and activities the United States uses to: engage with foreign partners and help shape their policies and actions in the security sector; help foreign partners build and sustain the capacity and effectiveness of legitimate institutions to provide security, safety, and justice for their people; and enable foreign partners to contribute to efforts that address common security challenges." The White House, Presidential Policy Directive/PPD-23, "Security Sector Assistance," April 5, 2013, 3.

[9] DOD defines "security cooperation" as "All Department of Defense interactions with foreign defense establishments to build defense relationships that promote specific U.S. security interests, develop allied and friendly military capabilities for self-defense and multinational operations, and provide U.S. forces with peacetime and contingency access to a host nation." U.S. Department of Defense, Joint Publication 1-02: *Dictionary of Military and Associated Terms*, March 15, 2013, 255.

[10] "Building partner capacity" should not be confused with "building partnership capacity," which DOD defines as "Targeted efforts to improve the collective capabilities and performance of the Department of Defense and its partners," with partners defined as other departments and agencies of the United States government, state and local governments, allies, coalition members, host nations, other nations, multinational organizations, non-governmental organizations, and the private sector. U.S. Department of Defense, *Building Partnership Capacity: QDR Execution Roadmap*, 2006, 4. By contrast, "building partner capacity" is a widely used phrase undefined in joint publications or other DOD guidance that refers to building the capabilities of a PN rather than the U.S. government.

[11] U.S. Air Force, *2011 USAF Global Partnership Strategy*, 18 and U.S. Air Force, *USAF Air Advising Operating Concept*, 8. These documents define "aviation enterprise" as "the sum total of all air domain resources, processes, and cultures...to include personnel, equipment, infrastructure, operations, sustainment, and air-mindedness."

[12] Air Force Doctrine Document 3-2: *Irregular Warfare*, March 15, 2013, 2.

In addition to conducting IW indirectly "by, with, and through" PNs in this way, the U.S. military also conducts IW directly through various operations. According to the IW JOC: "the principal way that the joint force will counter irregular threats in both steady-state and surge conditions is by some combination of counterterrorism, unconventional warfare [UW],[13] foreign internal defense [FID],[14] counterinsurgency [COIN],[15] and stability operations."[16] These are often referred to as the **"five pillars of IW."** These efforts must carefully balance population and threat-focused action and require extensive collaboration with non-DOD agencies, multinational partners, and PNs as well as continuous, coordinated cyberspace operations and messaging. They also require an in-depth understanding of the relevant operational environment (including history, culture, causes of conflict, and PN capabilities). Additional direct U.S. operations and activities used to counter irregular threats include information operations, civil-military operations, intelligence gathering, medical support, counterintelligence operations, and support to law enforcement.

Generally, IW campaigns require a combination of both direct and indirect IW operations. In addition, IW often is conducted during more traditional state-on-state conflicts. Therefore, the U.S. military must be prepared to simultaneously conduct both IW and traditional warfare.

Airpower Contributions to IW

Broadly speaking, airpower[17] extends PN reach and brings rapid response (both strike and lift) and improved situational awareness. These in turn help PNs establish the physical and virtual infrastructure essential for internal growth and well-being. Airpower

---

[13] DOD defines "unconventional warfare" as "Activities conducted to enable a resistance movement or insurgency to coerce, disrupt, or overthrow a government or occupying power by operating through or with an underground, auxiliary, and guerrilla force in a denied area…" U.S. Department of Defense, Joint Publication 1-02: *Dictionary of Military and Associated Terms*, March 15, 2013, 301.

[14] DOD defines "foreign internal defense" as "participation by civilian and military agencies of a government in any of the action programs taken by another government or other designated organization to free and protect its society from subversion, lawlessness, insurgency, terrorism, and other threats to its security." U.S. Department of Defense, Joint Publication 1-02: *Dictionary of Military and Associated Terms*, March 15, 2013, 113.

[15] DOD defines "counterinsurgency" as "comprehensive civilian and military efforts taken to defeat an insurgency and to address any core grievances." U.S. Department of Defense, Joint Publication 1-02: *Dictionary of Military and Associated Terms*, March 15, 2013, 65.

[16] The IW JOC also notes there is "significant overlap among the five activities, in particular between foreign internal defense, stability operations, and counterinsurgency. The former term came into being as a replacement for counterinsurgency in the decade after Vietnam, but it is now used more broadly to characterize support to another country facing insurgency or other forms of lawlessness and subversion. When foreign internal defense is conducted in low-threat environments, it shares many common features with stability operations. Finally, counterterrorism and unconventional warfare are evolving to include broader features than their core notions of defeating terrorists and using indigenous partners to overthrow state or state-like adversaries." U.S. Department of Defense, Chairman of the Joint Chiefs of Staff, *Irregular Warfare: Countering Irregular Threats Joint Operating Concept, Version 2.0*, May 17, 2010, 17.

[17] USAF doctrine defines "airpower" as "the ability to project military power or influence through the control and exploitation of air, space, and cyberspace to achieve strategic, operational, or tactical objectives." Air Force Doctrine Document 1: *Air Force Basic Doctrine, Organization, and Command*, October 14, 2011, 11.

also bolsters all instruments of national power and provides visible, practical, and effective means to consolidate governance and provide for the populace.

More specifically, airpower enables PNs to:

- Provide political leaders immediate, largely unimpeded access to all operational domains (air, land, sea, space, and cyberspace) to demonstrate governance and legitimacy by delivering goods, services, and humanitarian relief;

- Support military and civil ground forces in providing security and rapid response, developing infrastructure, and enhancing local governance;

- Deny adversaries unfettered access to ungoverned, under-governed, and remote areas;

- Patrol and help secure porous borders;

- Promote civil sector advancement, especially in air and cyberspace infrastructure;

- Deter and defeat external aggression;

- Inhibit hostile forces from moving openly or in large numbers without fear of detection and attack; and

- Strengthen internal security.

However, where insurgencies or other irregular challenges evolve to the point at which PNs can no longer face them on their own, U.S. airpower can be used directly to provide:[18]

- Global integrated intelligence, surveillance, and reconnaissance (ISR), particularly (1) cultural intelligence and popular perceptions using mostly non- USAF data and (2) ISR on small, hidden, and fleeting targets;

- Medical capability, to include patient movement;

- Mobility for armed forces;

- Command and control;

- Global precision strike (while keeping the effect of such strikes on the population's perception of the PN's legitimacy at the forefront);

- Agile combat support (particularly to remote, austere bases with extended supply lines and limited communications), which includes airbase opening, airbase defense, area security operations, and aviation-related civil engineering;

- Assistance against improvised explosive devices, weapons of mass destruction, mines, and other unexploded ordnance;

- Humanitarian assistance and disaster relief;

- Military information support operations;

- Personnel recovery and evacuation, including non-combatants;

---

[18] For more details, refer to Air Force Doctrine Document 3-2: *Irregular Warfare*, March 15, 2013, 33-43.

- Close air support;

- Electronic warfare;

- Information operations;

- Communications synchronization;

- Offensive and defensive cyberspace operations;

- Offensive and defensive counter-space operations; and

- Global space mission operations.

Updated National Guidance on IW

The national guidance that existed when the original USAF IW Strategy was published in 2009 already emphasized the importance of and the need for IW capabilities in the U.S. military. More specifically, the 2008 *National Defense Strategy* **directed the U.S. military to: (1) become as proficient in IW as it is in conventional warfare; and (2) to focus on building, strengthening, and expanding partnerships with nations** to achieve *National Security Strategy* goals of countering terrorism, preventing crises from escalating into conflict, and securing U.S. strategic access and freedom of action. In addition, the 2006 *Quadrennial Defense Review Report*:

- Tasked the development of an IW Roadmap and a Building Partnership Capacity Roadmap for DOD;

- Advocated additional funding for language and cultural skills;

- Incorporated IW and building partner capacity into the DOD Force Planning Construct; and

- Advocated increasing IW topics in joint training and training of PN military personnel in U.S. professional military education institutions.

Furthermore, DOD published IW guidance in 2008[19] that directed the Services, among other things, to:

- Maintain military capabilities and track the capacity and proficiency of the Military Services to meet combatant commander (CCDR) IW-related requirements in accordance with strategic guidance documents; and

- Maintain scalable organizations to train and advise foreign security forces and security institutions (unilaterally or as part of civilian-military teams) in permissive and uncertain environments

---

[19] U.S. Department of Defense, DOD Directive 3000.07 - *Irregular Warfare*, 2008, 8.

Since then, the President of the United States and the DOD have published a new *National Security Strategy, Quadrennial Defense Review Report* (both in 2010), a new Defense Strategic Guidance entitled *Sustaining U.S. Global Leadership: Priorities for 21st Century Defense* (in 2012), and a new Presidential Policy Directive/PPD-23 entitled *Security Sector Assistance*, (in 2013). These documents build on their predecessors to provide additional and more detailed strategic guidance associated with IW. More specifically, this new guidance:

- Emphasizes non-military means and military-to-military cooperation over direct U.S. military operations to address instability and reduce the demand for significant U.S. force commitments to stability operations;

- Lists counterterrorism, IW, stability operations, COIN operations, and providing a stabilizing presence (in part to enhance building partner capacity) among the "primary missions" of the U.S. military;

- Elevates the importance of relying on innovative, low-cost, and small-footprint approaches such as advisory capabilities to achieve U.S. national security objectives;

- Rebalances IW efforts from the large-scale COIN and stability operations in Iraq and Afghanistan (and deemphasizing such operations as a sizing construct for U.S. forces) to a more distributed effort around the globe characterized by "a mix of direct action and security force assistance [SFA]"[20];

- Emphasizes the need to prioritize the location and frequency of operations associated with presence operations abroad (to include SSA) given reduced resources;

- Emphasizes the need to invest in "capable partners of the future";

- Prioritizes the goal of enabling PNs to provide for their own security, contribute effectively to broader regional or global security challenges, and maintain professional, civilian-led militaries that respect human rights;

- Instructs Services to strengthen and institutionalize general purpose forces (GPF) SC capabilities;

- Rebalances DOD efforts overall towards the Asia-Pacific region; and

- Emphasizes need to strengthen capacity to plan, synchronize, and implement SSA through a deliberate and inclusive whole-of-government process that ensures alignment of activities and resources with national security priorities.

---

[20] DOD defines "security force assistance" as "The Department of Defense activities that contribute to unified action by the U.S. Government to support the development of the capacity and capability of foreign security forces and their supporting institutions." U.S. Department of Defense, Joint Publication 1-02: *Dictionary of Military and Associated Terms*, March 15, 2013, 256. SFA is a subset of security cooperation.

As a result, the *Guidance for Employment of the Force* (GEF)[21] notes "contingency plans tasked by the President in the GEF are considered 'branches' to the GEF-tasked campaign plans. As such, contingency plans must first address prevention and deterrence of the contingencies. Contingency plans are built to account for the possibility that shaping measures, SC activities, and other DOD operations could fail to prevent aggression, preclude large-scale instability in a key state or region, or mitigate the effects of a major disaster."[22]

OSD has also erected a new analytic framework to assess the Services' fiscal year (FY) 2014 spending proposals and accompanying five-year investment blueprints, establishing various strategic portfolios (including SFA) to identify capability gaps and potential redundancies.

Shortfalls and Challenges Affecting USAF IW

Also since the initial USAF IW Strategy was published in 2009, the IW Capabilities Based Assessment Campaign, the 2009 USAF CORONA South, the USAF IW Tiger Team report, various USAF core function master plans, and a USAF study conducted by RAND Corporation[23] have documented significant shortfalls and challenges affecting USAF IW operations – many of which are outside the USAF's direct control. These challenges, which hinder the USAF's ability to address the new IW strategic guidance, are briefly listed below (and detailed in Appendix D):

- There is a lack of a coordinated strategy, process, or plan to conduct IW across the whole-of-government.

- IW-related authorities often hinder effective long-term planning and execution.

- Many PNs cannot afford, fly, or sustain current USAF weapons systems.

- IW planning is complicated by the lack of a consistently articulated demand signal from the combatant commands, U.S. embassies, and associated strategic plans.

- Building partner capacity has not traditionally been a designed operational capability requirement, even for units regularly involved with PNs.

- The USAF's force providers and personnel system are not optimized for, nor do they have sufficient personnel needed by, the geographic CCDRs to effectively plan, execute, conduct, and support effective IW.

- The USAF lacks adequate IW training and education.

---

[21] The stated purpose of the GEF is to translate national security objectives and high-level strategy into DOD priorities and comprehensive planning direction to guide the Department's components in the employment of forces. OSD produces the GEF.

[22] U.S. Department of Defense, *2012 Guidance For Employment of the Force*, 4-5.

[23] Moroney, Jennifer, et al, *International Cooperation with Partner Air Forces* (RAND Corporation, Santa Monica, CA, 2009).

- The USAF Service core function master plans and the integrated priorities lists of the CCDRs describe various shortfalls affecting the ability of the USAF to conduct effective direct IW operations.

- The organizational structures of special operations forces, GPF, and other government agencies limit planning integration and synchronization across the whole-of-government and enduring distributed operations.

3. USAF IW STRATEGY TO IMPLEMENT NEW STRATEGIC GUIDANCE

The USAF IW strategy to organize, train, and equip to address the current strategic guidance concerning IW and the documented challenges affecting the USAF's ability to achieve that guidance is to:

1 - Adopt a Partnering Culture

The USAF strongly supports the OSD push to "develop a 'partnering culture.'"[24] Airmen across the Total Force must culturally understand that security cooperation to build partner capacity is not some distraction from their fundamental mission, but part of it.

Going forward, air advising and being an instructor to partner air forces and civilian aviation will be part of the fundamental identity, self-concept, and expectations of individual Airmen. Building and maintaining language, region, and culture expertise; demonstrating air advising skills; and thinking strategically about how peacetime operations can shape geopolitical relationships to provide advantage for U.S. foreign policy will grow in importance and positively affect individual promotions.

Our expectation going forward is that Airmen will be intellectual thought leaders and bring ideas about how to employ not just the destructive effects of airpower, but also its constructive effects – deterrence, dissuasion, assurance, humanitarian assistance/disaster relief, building partnerships, air diplomacy, and partner aviation enterprise development (AED) – to service national security and foreign policy needs.

Implementing the goals in the *USAF IW Operations Roadmap* (described later) related to: (1) establishing air advisor institutional capability in the GPF; (2) training Airmen to be equally proficient and capable in irregular and conventional warfare operations; and (3) educating Airmen to be proficient and capable leaders in irregular and conventional warfare should greatly enhance this effort.

---

[24] Secretary of Defense Leon E. Panetta speech at the U.S. Institute of Peace, Washington, DC; June 28, 2012.

2 - *Influence U.S. Global Shaping Activities Guided by a New USAF Aviation Enterprise Development Vision and Strategy*

As previously discussed, the primary USAF approach to conduct IW indirectly by, with, and through PNs is to help develop, enhance, and sustain their aviation enterprise as directed by the Department of State as part of the overall U.S. SSA effort. Such U.S. assistance of PN AED efforts is conducted across the U.S. government (not just by the USAF or DOD) and cover a wide range of areas impacting both the civilian and security sectors of PNs: professional military education; assessing, training, and advising personnel throughout the aviation domain; educating military and civilian leadership about the value of airpower; constructing, operating, securing, and maintaining airfields; operating air traffic control; establishing effective terminal procedures as well as cargo and passenger movement operations; achieving air and maritime domain awareness; enhancing airport personnel and cargo security; providing aviation support (logistics, supply, maintenance, aerospace medicine, human performance factors, etc.); enhancing air-land integration; providing survival and search and rescue training; developing an industrial and research base; and improving staff planning, collaborative planning, and budgeting.

The United States has been assisting the AED of PNs for years. However, other than the Aviation FID missions conducted by the Air Force Special Operations Command, it generally has been ad hoc and short-term reactions to crises and current needs as opposed to a deliberate, proactive, long-term planning effort aligned to long-term U.S. strategic interests.[25] In part, this is because the United States lacks a vision and strategy to guide and inform long-term, sustained SSA or AED across the whole-of-government. The recently published PPD-23 intends to address this by requiring the National Security Staff to develop and issue national-level guidance for SSA on a biennial basis and creating an interagency SSA Oversight Board co-chaired by the Departments of State and Defense to ensure U.S. government SSA efforts are executed in a timely, coordinated, and effective manner.

While the USAF is only one of many actors conducting and influencing PN AED efforts abroad and does not lead them per strategic guidance, it has clear equities in the whole-of-government effort, especially given it is a critical enabler of future base access vital to achieving global vigilance, reach, and power.[26] Therefore, the Secretary of the Air Force and the Chief of Staff of the Air Force have tasked the USAF through the *USAF IW Operations Roadmap* to "develop a vision and strategy for global partnership aviation enterprise development...to inform HQ USAF inputs to [Air Force Forces] AFFOR,

---

[25] PPD-23 notes that American SSA investments must be "strategic and focused on investments aligned with national security priorities and in countries where the conditions are right for sustained progress."

[26] In the foreword of the *USAF Global Partnership Strategy*, the Chief of Staff and Secretary of the Air Force observe, "We can't have Global Vigilance, Reach, and Power for America without Global Partnerships."

[CCDRs], and OSD Strategy."[27] In addition to shaping the PPD-23 mandated efforts above, a USAF AED Vision and Strategy would also shape:

- Investments by the U.S. government, industry, and global financial institutions on global aviation infrastructure;

- U.S. diplomatic efforts that could increase USAF engagement and global access;

- Resource allocation by agencies that have responsive ideas and vision for peacetime global shaping; and

- Strategic plans by combatant commands and OSD to ensure air, space, and cyberspace equities.

It is the intent of the USAF AED Vision and Strategy to serve as a starting point for discussion for the whole-of-government AED effort and lead to a very similar document that would be published under an interagency banner as a 3D (development, diplomacy, and defense) strategy for shaping the global air domain.

3 - Advocate IW Authorities That Enable Effective, Long-Term, Persistent Engagements

As highlighted in Appendix D and the 2011 *National Military Strategy of the United States*, the laws governing SSA efforts across the U.S. government and the lack of broad authority for multi-year spending creates a confusing and difficult patchwork of authorities that prevents effective long-term planning essential for most IW operations and activities and required by strategic guidance. This authority patchwork therefore generates missed opportunities to build partner capacity in high priority nations defined by the GEF, opportunities sometimes filled by other nations as a result.

PPD-23's implementation memo tasks departments and agencies to review existing legal authorities to determine if there are modifications needed to meet current demands and policy guidance, and seek to amend authorities that are unresponsive to departments' and agencies' requirements. If needed, departments and agencies may propose new authorities for consideration to enhance United States Government capabilities and capacity to implement SSA priorities. The USAF will continue to work with Congress and OSD and all relevant organizations to address or mitigate this challenge through legislation and other appropriate means.

---

[27] U.S. Air Force, *United States Air Force Irregular Warfare Operations Roadmap FY12 – FY15*, October 2012, 12.

4 - Establish the Means to Meet Global Light Aviation Demands with American Aircraft and Services

As USAF IW doctrine notes, IW is about "right-tech," not about high- or low-tech.[28] A USAF goal is to position itself to be the light aviation advising, assisting, and training partner of choice for its foreign allies and partners through a combination of general purpose and special operations forces aviation capabilities.[29] As discussed in more detail in Appendix D, the lack of USAF platforms that PNs can afford, operate, and sustain is a significant challenge to ongoing SC efforts, especially in AED.

The 2010 *Quadrennial Defense Review Report* tasked the USAF to "field light mobility and light attack aircraft in general purpose force units in order to increase their ability to work effectively with a wider range of partner air forces."[30] In the current climate of declining budgets and numerous priorities, however, the USAF has been unable to acquire and maintain its own separate, specialized light aviation force structure. Therefore, the USAF will establish a creative, effective, and affordable way to enhance its ability to develop PN air forces that use light aircraft.

Potential options include, but are not limited to: (1) using the existing Foreign Military Sales and SC infrastructure as a conduit for force structure employed by the USAF Auxiliary, Air Reserve Components, civilian agencies, and law enforcement already performing comparable internal security missions with more applicable and affordable equipment; (2) the purchase of a handful of very basic, inexpensive "off-the-shelf" light aircraft to be attached to existing advisory units; (3) novel partnerships with contract service providers or civilian agencies to allow Airmen to gain and maintain proficiency in light aircraft in an internal security role; and/or (4) the use of current and future U.S. trainer aircraft for this purpose where appropriate.

5 - Adequately Man Planning Staffs Associated With IW

To effectively execute IW-related strategic guidance and elements of this USAF IW strategy, there must not only be adequately trained personnel on planning staffs (particularly those AFFOR staffs supporting the geographic CCDRs), but also enough personnel to effectively plan and execute IW, especially in drafting and executing long-term country plans. Planning staff levels today often cannot keep up with the demands of day-to-day operations and interactions with other nations, much less perform effective long-term planning that will only increase over time as the DOD shifts to a more deliberate planning system that creates long-term country and regional strategies.

---

[28] Air Force Doctrine Document 3-2: *Irregular Warfare,* March 15, 2013, 11.

[29] The Defense Strategic Guidance states: "Across the globe we will seek to be the security partner of choice, pursuing new partnerships with a growing number of nations — including those in Africa and Latin America — whose interests and viewpoints are merging into a common vision of freedom, stability, and prosperity. Whenever possible, we will develop innovative, low-cost, and small-footprint approaches to achieve our security objectives, relying on exercises, rotational presence, and advisory capabilities." U.S. Department of Defense, *Sustaining U.S. Global Leadership: Priorities for 21st Century Defense, January 2012,* 3.

[30] U.S. Department of Defense. *Quadrennial Defense Review Report, February 2010,* 29.

In order of priority, the USAF will address this shortfall by: (1) filling current authorized billets on planning staffs associated with IW; (2) increasing manpower billets on planning staffs associated with IW to align with the new responsibilities associated with SC; (3) internally rebalancing billets on planning staffs to maximize the manpower tied to IW planning without taking unacceptable risk in other areas; (4) when possible and appropriate, taking advantage of the personnel across the Total Force; and (5) formalizing the annual transition of AFFOR-developed campaign support plans to the A3 and/or the Air Operations Center for execution, allowing planners to focus on long-term planning and assessment instead of execution. As much as possible, these billets should be filled with the most qualified personnel available.

6 - *Excel at IW-Related Planning, Resourcing, Execution, and Assessment*

The Theater Campaign Plan provides the direction and prioritization for U.S. military forces to achieve the strategic objectives of the geographic CCDR. USAF component commanders, in turn, develop Commander, Air Force Forces (COMAFFOR) Campaign Support Plans and USAF Country Support Plans to document the specific actions USAF will undertake in support of the Theater Campaign Plan. These plans combine the effort of each individual Service component commander and PN force as well as Department of State country teams and various other interagency organizations. These USAF steady-state plans are different from other deliberate plans in that they are executed to the degree that resources can be attracted. The execution of these plans must also be assessed.

The COMAFFOR Campaign Support Plan and USAF Country Support Plans also provide a CCDR-validated demand signal to inform USAF organize, train, and equip decision-making associated with IW and SC. Not only does this demand signal influence resource allocation, but it also influences capability-based planning for IW and SC. The USAF capability to plan, resource, execute, and assess the COMAFFOR Campaign Support Plan is slowly improving, but is hampered by inadequate USAF policy, guidance, doctrine, and training.

Properly developed and executed long-term Theater Campaign Plans, Campaign Support Plans, and Country Support Plans that effectively consider the full spectrum of IW activities (to include SC and AED) at a sufficient level of detail are critical to enable the Service resourcing and manpower processes to address IW-related needs and shortfalls. Such plans must articulate the long-term demand for trained and dedicated air advisors to perform SC missions and identify gaps in qualified air advisor capabilities.

As directed by PPD-23, Airmen, including regional specialists, operational planners, defense attachés, SC officers, component numbered Air Forces, and CCDR staff elements, will continually engage in this process with all involved (especially PN leadership, the Department of State, CCDRs, the other Services, and key allies) to ensure air, space, and cyberspace power are effectively integrated into these plans.

7 - Develop a USAF Concept and Strategy Using GPF to Support UW

Whereas the IW pillars of FID, counterterrorism, stability operations, and COIN all position the United States on the side of the incumbent government, UW positions the United States on the side of the insurgents. While UW is a specific competency and mission area of special operations forces, it has been supported by GPF in recent conflicts such as Kosovo, Afghanistan, and Libya, albeit on an ad hoc basis. UW is a joint operation involving the whole-of-government and capabilities across all the domains. There are foreseeable conflicts ahead where the United States may need to call on indigenous or surrogate forces to conduct operations to aid in an air, space, and cyberspace domain control campaign. Therefore, it is important that Airmen think through the future use of UW in advance and promote early consideration of airpower as appropriate in joint and interagency thinking. Such efforts would also support the Joint Requirements Oversight Council Memorandum tasks to both enable understanding of UW and its utility as a strategic option and improve the ability to support UW.

To meet strategic guidance given expected future operating environments, the USAF will develop a UW concept and strategy that, among other things: (1) integrates GPF; (2) integrates into the overall USAF and DOD strategy; (3) transcends both functional and regional combatant commands; (4) integrates external capabilities across the joint force and other agencies; (5) effectively guides deliberate planning and capability development related to UW; (6) ensures effectiveness in anti-access/area-denial environments; (7) captures lessons learned from recent airpower-indigenous force teaming; (8) effectively incorporates UW, where appropriate, to assist overall USAF air, space, and cyberspace operations; and (9) supports efforts to develop joint doctrine on UW.

8 - Address USAF Shortfalls in Conducting Direct IW Operations

Nearly all USAF capabilities can be used to conduct or support direct IW operations. The USAF Service core function master plans and CCDR integrated priorities lists describe (mostly at the classified level) various shortfalls in the ability of the USAF to conduct effective direct IW operations. Therefore, it is important for the Air Force Corporate Structure to evaluate and prioritize those shortfalls within the USAF POM.

9 - Implement the USAF IW Operations Roadmap FY12-FY16

The *USAF IW Operations Roadmap* lists a number of tasks intended to: (1) achieve the same level of proficiency in IW as conventional warfare; (2) institutionalize IW across the USAF; and (3) address a number of identified materiel and non-materiel IW shortfalls. Together, these tasks, which are administered by the USAF IW Task Force, are intended to achieve the following goals:

- Develop USAF doctrine, concepts, as well as tactics, techniques, and procedures that describe and guide air, space, and cyberspace forces in activities and operations to counter irregular threats and those activities supporting SC and SFA.

- Establish air advising institutional capability in the GPF by maintaining units organized, trained, and equipped to present expeditionary capabilities for IW as part of properly trained, forward-based GPF units, contingency response forces, air expeditionary GPF units, or Air National Guard units participating with the National Guard Bureau State Partnership Program. Forces will be scaled or task-organized to meet CCDR requests for forces.

- Train Airmen to be equally proficient and capable in irregular and conventional warfare operations.

- Equip Airmen for countering irregular threats and building the capacity of the security forces of willing PNs.

- Educate Airmen to be proficient and capable leaders in irregular and conventional warfare.

- Design well-defined air advising qualifications and abilities, to include training, force management, force development, and career path perspectives.

- Provide guidance to Airmen on how USAF will track personnel capacity and proficiency in IW and SFA related requirements.

- Develop USAF issuances (instructions, manuals, and pamphlets) to provide guidance and instruction for Airmen engaging in operations against irregular threats and supporting aviation enterprise SFA.

Please refer to the *USAF IW Operations Roadmap* for details. Implementing the tasks of the *USAF IW Operations Roadmap* as well as the ongoing "IW [Capabilities Based Assessment] Campaign DOTMLPF Change Recommendation Joint Requirements Oversight Council Memorandum" Assigned Tasks[31] will improve USAF IW capabilities and operations.

---

[31] The *2006 QDR Execution Roadmap for Irregular Warfare* required the development of IW JOC 1.0, from which three Joint Integrating Concepts were developed: UW, FID, and Defeat Terrorist Networks. Several Joint Capabilities Integration and Development System documents followed the concept development stages of the campaign, including seven Doctrine, Organization, Training, Materiel, Leadership and Education, Personnel, and Facilities (DOTMLPF) Change Recommendations and two Initial Capability Documents. The implementation of these recommendations, which would improve USAF IW capabilities and operations, is still ongoing. These IW-related recommendations have generated over 120 Joint Requirements Oversight Council Memorandum tasks.

4. CONCLUSION

In summary, this updated USAF IW Strategy provides direction for the USAF to organize, train, and equip to execute strategic guidance related to IW. Together, its initiatives will:

- Address materiel and non-materiel shortfalls that inhibit USAF efforts to effectively conduct IW in support of US strategic interests;

- Improve USAF deliberate, long-term planning for IW;

- Influence and improve whole-of-government efforts to build partner capacity, as their success is critical to enabling access to conduct global air, space, and cyberspace operations in the future; and

- Improve the chances that nations important to American interests will partner with the United States as opposed to strategic competitors.

In turn, these efforts will put the USAF in a strong position to address strategic guidance on IW to support U.S. security interests by helping to rebalance IW:

- From large-scale operations to low-cost, small footprint approaches;

- From direct U.S. operations to indirect actions by, with, and through PNs;

- From large-scale COIN and stability operations in Iraq and Afghanistan to a more distributed, though carefully prioritized, global effort focusing more on the Asia-Pacific region;

- From crisis response, near-term focused efforts to more deliberative, long-term efforts closely tied to enduring U.S. strategic interests; and

- From predominantly a special operations force mission to one institutionalized across the general purpose force.

APPENDIX A – USAF EFFORTS TO INSTITUTIONALIZE AND ENHANCE IRREGULAR WARFARE SINCE THE INITIAL USAF IW STRATEGY IN 2009

Some of these efforts, listed in no particular order, may be scaled back or eliminated by anticipated defense cuts:

- Established detailed guidance regarding language, region, and cultural proficiency levels within the USAF's Manpower Programming and Execution System;

- Established the Air Advisor Academy, which has trained over 2,000 personnel to be expeditionary advisors;

- Established the Language Enabled Airman Program, a pilot program to give select Airmen thorough language and cultural education and training to create a cadre of willing and capable GPF Airmen to meet future SC requirements;

- Established the USAF Steady-State Campaign Support Planners' Course;

- Instituted an annual Air Force Campaign Support Plan;

- Repurposed 5,600 active duty billets over the Future Years Defense Program to support ISR capability, U.S. Pacific Command force structure requirements, Total Force Integration, and SC;

- Transitioned the MC-12W Liberty Project from Overseas Contingency Operations funding into the USAF baseline budget beginning in FY 2014;

- Recapitalized the MC-130E, MC-130P, and AC-130H aircraft;

- Increased USAF Global Health Engagement activities;

- Increased Air National Guard and USAF budgetary support to the National Guard Bureau's State Partnership Program;

- Increased dedicated GPF for SC through contingency response forces in Air Mobility Command, Pacific Air Forces, and U.S. Air Forces Europe;

- Published numerous policy; doctrine; strategic planning; concepts of employment; concepts of operation; tactics, techniques, and procedures; and planning order publications related to IW (see Appendix B for a detailed list);

- Continued to expand the Inter-American Air Forces Academy, which focuses on building partner capacity through educating and training aviation forces from Latin America in Spanish in a wide variety of technical, operational, doctrinal, and procedural skills;

- Continued maximum production of the MQ-9 Reaper to ensure 65 combat air patrols by the end of FY 2014;

- Continued to command and field Joint Provincial Reconstruction Teams in Afghanistan and Iraq conducting governance, security, and development missions outside the wire; and

- Established the Air Force Special Operations Air Warfare Center to organize, train, and equip forces to conduct special operations missions; lead Air Force Special Operations Command IW activities; execute special operations test and evaluation and lessons learned programs; and develop doctrine, tactics, techniques, and procedures for USAF special operations in the IW environment.

APPENDIX B – KEY IRREGULAR WARFARE POLICY, DOCTRINE, AND CONCEPT PUBLICATIONS

President of the United States:
- *National Security Strategy* (2010)
- Presidential Policy Directive/PPD-23, *Security Sector Assistance* (2013)

Secretary of Defense:
- DOD Directive 3000.07, *Irregular Warfare* (2008)
- DOD Directive 5100.01, *Functions of the Department of Defense and Its Major Components* (2010)
- DOD Directive 5132.03, *DoD Policy and Responsibilities Relating to Security Cooperation* (2008)
- DOD Directive 5132.12, *Consolidations and Reductions of U.S. Defense Attaché Offices (DAOs) and Security Assistance Organizations (SAOs)*, 1991 (certified updated in 2003)
- DOD Instruction 2010.12, *Aviation Leadership Program* (2008)
- DOD Instruction 3000.05, *Stability Operations* (2009)
- DOD Instruction 5000.68, *Security Force Assistance* (2010)
- DOD Instruction 5410.17, *United States Field Studies Program (FSP) for International Military and Civilian Students and Military-Sponsored Visitors* (2008)
- *Guidance for Employment of the Force* (2012)
- *National Defense Strategy* (2008)
- *Quadrennial Defense Review Report* (2010)
- *Sustaining U.S. Global Leadership: Priorities for 21st Century Defense* (2012)

Chairman of the Joint Chiefs of Staff:
- CJCS Instruction 3210.06, *Irregular Warfare* (2010)
- *Foreign Internal Defense* Joint Integrating Concept (2010)
- *Irregular Warfare: Countering Irregular Threats Joint Operating Concept – Version 2.0* (2010)
- Joint Publication 3-0, *Joint Operations* (2011)
- Joint Publication 3-07, *Stability Operations* (2011)
- Joint Publication 3-22, *Foreign Internal Defense* (2010)
- Joint Publication 3-24, *Counterinsurgency Operations* (2009)

- Joint Publication 3-26, *Counterterrorism* (2009)

- Joint Publication 5-0, *Joint Operation Planning* (2011)

USAF

- *Air Combat Command IW Operating Concept* (2008)

- *Air Combat Command Light Attack/Armed Reconnaissance (LAAR) Squadron Concept of Employment* (2010)

- Air Force Doctrine Document 3-2, *Irregular Warfare* (2013)

- Air Force Doctrine Document 3-22, *Foreign Internal Defense* (2007 – last reviewed in 2011)

- Air Force Instruction 16-122, *Security Force Assistance* (2012) (implements DOD Instruction 5000.68)

- Air Force Policy Directive 10-42, *Irregular Warfare* (2011) (implements DOD Directive 3000.07)

- Air Force Policy Directive 10-43, *Stability Operations* (2011) (implements DOD Instruction 3000.05)

- Air Force Policy Directive 16-1, *International Affairs* (2009) (implements DOD Directive 5132.03, DOD Directive 5132.12, DOD Directive 5230.20, DOD Instruction 2010.12, and DOD Instruction 5410.17)

- Air Force Policy Directive 36-40, *Air Force Language, Region & Culture Program* (2012) (implements DOD Directive 5160.41E)

- *Air Force Space Command Irregular Warfare Engagement Plan* (2010)

- Air Force Tactics, Techniques, and Procedures 3-2.76, *Advising Multi-Service Tactics, Techniques, and Procedures for Advising Foreign Forces* (2009)

- Air Force Tactics, Techniques, and Procedures 3-4.5, *Air Advising* (2012)

- *Planning Order for the 2013 USAF Campaign Support Plan 0800-13* (2012)

- *USAF Air Advising Operating Concept: Version 1.0* (2012)

- *USAF Building Partnerships Core Function Master Plan FY 15* (2012)

- *USAF Global Partnership Strategy* (2011)

- *USAF IW Operating Concept* (2008)

- *USAF Irregular Warfare Operations Roadmap FY12-FY16* (2012)

- *USAF IW Tiger Team: Observations and Recommendations* (2009)

- *USAF Security Cooperation Engagement Guidance For the Air Domain* (2012)

- *USAF Strategic Environmental Assessment, 2010-2030* (2010)

APPENDIX C – SUMMARY OF FUTURE GLOBAL TRENDS ASSOCIATED WITH IRREGULAR WARFARE

According to the consensus of the intelligence and military communities summarized in the *USAF Strategic Environmental Assessment, 2010-2030,* the rise of irregular challenges have been driven by the following trends and developments, which are expected to continue for at least the next twenty years:

- The conventional superiority of U.S. forces is forcing most potential adversaries to seek more non-traditional "asymmetric" (to include irregular) means.

- Both state and non-state actors (including irregular challengers such as terrorists, transnational groups and criminals, individuals, and insurgents) are acquiring or developing the means to challenge U.S. military power and global interests and directly threaten the U.S. homeland as:

  o Globalization reduces barriers to free movement of goods, people, information, services, ideas, and money;

  o Dual use technologies increase; and

  o Enrollment of students in the universities of advanced nations increases.

- Many regions and PNs are becoming more unstable due to various global trends:

  o Globalization's broad sharing of information is enabling populations and individuals to challenge their governments;

  o Globalization's economic benefits have been uneven between states and within states;

  o Globalization has reduced barriers between formerly insular cultures and the rest of the world and thus has been widely perceived as a threat to traditional values;

  o Demographic changes have created large migration patterns from poor to wealthy nations and from rural to urban areas within nations;

  o Distribution of energy, water, and food is growing more uneven;

  o Global climate change is altering the location of arable land, water availability, sea levels, and access to natural resources;

  o Many developing areas of the world are experiencing rapid population growth, outpacing the ability of those economies to create enough jobs and provide basic services and resources; and

  o The threat of pandemics and other local infectious diseases are growing.

In turn, the demand on U.S. forces to conduct IW, urban operations, humanitarian operations, and special operations will likely continue to increase into the foreseeable future. In addition, deterrence is expected to become more challenging, especially vis-à-vis non-state actors often associated with IW.

APPENDIX D –SHORTFALLS AND CHALLENGES AFFECTING USAF IW OPERATIONS

Since the initial USAF IW Strategy was published in 2009, the IW JOC's Capabilities Based Assessment, the 2009 USAF CORONA, the USAF IW Tiger Team report, various USAF core function master plans, and a USAF study conducted by RAND Corporation[32] have documented significant shortfalls and challenges affecting the USAF's ability to address new strategic guidance concerning IW. These shortfalls and challenges, which are mostly out of the USAF's control, are briefly discussed below:

- **There is a lack of a coordinated strategy, process, or plan to conduct IW across the whole-of-government.** Both DOD guidance and USAF doctrine emphasize that conducting successful IW requires a unity of effort across all U.S. government instruments of power. While various parts of the U.S. government have developed strategies and plans to conduct IW, there is a lack of a coordinated strategy, process, or plan to conduct IW across the whole-of-government, particularly indirect IW such as SC to build partner capacity in a way that uses scarce resources most effectively to directly support long-term U.S. strategic interests.

- **IW-related authorities often hinder effective long-term planning and execution.** Such funding authority challenges have been well documented by the Government Accountability Office[33] and the *National Military Strategy of the United States*[34] as well as the geographic CCDRs through congressional testimony[35] and a meeting with the President in 2009.[36] For example:

  o The laws governing SSA efforts across the U.S. government and the lack of broad authority for multi-year spending creates a confusing and difficult patchwork of authorities that prevents the effective long-term planning essential for most IW efforts and required by strategic guidance. This authority patchwork generates missed opportunities to build partner capacity in high priority nations, opportunities sometimes filled by other nations as a result.

---

[32] Moroney, Jennifer, et al, *International Cooperation with Partner Air Forces* (RAND Corporation, Santa Monica, CA, 2009).

[33] See U.S. Government Accountability Office reports "Defense Management: Improved Planning, Training, and Interagency Collaboration Could Strengthen DOD's Efforts in Africa" (GAO-1-794, July 2010) and "Southeast Asia: Better Human Rights Reviews and Strategic Planning Needed for U.S. Assistance to Foreign Security Forces" (GAO-05-093, July 2005).

[34] Chairman of the Joint Chiefs of Staff, *The Military Strategy of the United States of America 2011: Redefining America's Military Leadership*, 15-16.

[35] For example, see Appendix A of Thomas Livingston, "Building the Capacity of Partner States Through Security Force Assistance," Washington, DC: Congressional Research Service, May 5, 2011.

[36] U.S. Department of Defense briefing entitled "Security Sector Assistance (SSA): Presidential Policy Directive (PPD) Overview & Next Steps," May 7, 2013, slide 2.

- o GPF may only conduct advise and assist training under special regional or country-specific authorities (e.g., Iraq Security Forces Fund or Afghanistan Security Forces Fund) or security assistance programs. In regions or countries without special authorities, GPF training opportunities with foreign security forces or supporting institutions are usually limited to participation in combined exercises with foreign military forces.

- o The fact some PNs employ foreign-built aircraft limits and complicates USAF engagement opportunities under existing authorities.

- o A DOD memorandum to the National Security Council [37] added that existing authorities:
    - Have not changed foreign military financing funding between 1991-2008;
    - Have short (about three years) budget-to-execution timelines that are not responsive to a changing security environment;
    - Are based on a security assistance framework designed for building long-term partnerships against a Cold War adversary; and
    - Are unclear about appropriate Title 10 and Title 22 programs in the area between war and peace.

- **Many PNs cannot afford, fly, or sustain current USAF weapons systems.** The aviation needs of many developing nations are quite different from those of nations with advanced militaries. They often simply need to learn basic airmanship, gain experience with maintenance and operations, and obtain and operate aircraft that more closely resemble what the United States uses for customs, border protection, and law enforcement as opposed to advanced combat. The highest PN demand is usually for light mobility and ISR platforms, with some demand for light attack platforms. Airplanes and airports are complex systems. When a nation purchases either, it is buying into a multi-decade relationship and influence with the seller nation. Unfortunately, because the United States (especially the USAF) today is not flying the types of platforms PNs need that are transferrable, affordable, modular, and interoperable, their primary alternative is to approach other suppliers. Therefore, the United States is missing significant shaping opportunities emphasized in strategic guidance.

- **Many planning staffs lack enough manpower to effectively plan, execute, and support IW, especially drafting and executing long-term country plans.** To effectively execute IW-related strategic guidance and elements of this USAF IW strategy, there must not only be adequately trained personnel on planning staffs (particularly those USAF staffs supporting the geographic CCDRs), but also

---

[37] Memorandum for Assistant to the President for National Security Affairs, "Subject: DOD Review of Building the Security Capacity of Partner Nations," June 18, 2009.

enough personnel to plan and execute IW and peacetime engagement, especially in drafting and executing long-term country plans. This results in situations where desk officers are planning for and trying to interact with more countries than they can realistically manage on top of trying to keep up with the demands of day-to-day operations. Appropriate manning is essential to achieving the strategic payoff of proper operational planning. This shortfall will only increase over time as the DOD shifts to a more deliberate planning system that creates long-term country and regional strategies.

- **IW planning is complicated by the lack of a consistently articulated demand signal from the combatant commands, U.S. embassies, and associated strategic master plans.** Such a long-term, consistent demand signal is necessary to train and educate enough personnel with the necessary regional, cultural, and language skills. Key leader engagements, theater exercises, and internal defense and development[38] plans all convey a demand signal by PNs. This demand signal, however, is not consistently articulated in the processes and documents that drive Service funding and manpower decisions in support of these activities. The USAF IW Tiger Team Report notes, "CCDRs and air components had two kinds of demand: specified and unspecified. Specified demand consists of the capabilities needed in the current IW and [building partner capacity] efforts in the [U.S. Central Command] arena, manning and training on CCDR staffs, and CCDR demand for [6th Special Operations Squadron] capability. Unspecified demand is hidden or suppressed, and consists of latent aviation IW, [building partner capacity], and [air advisor] capabilities that are unrequested or unidentified (RAND Project Air Force, *USAF and Train/Advise/Assist: How Much Is Enough?*). USAF organizations and potential partners, both within and outside the U.S. government, fail to make requests for USAF capabilities, because they are either unaware of existing capabilities or assume their requests will go unfulfilled. It is difficult to quantify this unspecified demand, though it is larger than the specified demand; the request for forces…process cannot be used as an empirical measure of demand, because component planners do not often use this process to fill IW, [building partner capacity], and [air advisor] requirements."[39] Future USAF Campaign Support Plans intend to develop, consolidate, and prioritize an USAF SC demand signal for USAF strategic planning and programming.

---

[38] DOD defines "internal defense and development" as "the full range of measures taken by a nation to promote its growth and to protect itself from subversion, lawlessness, insurgency, terrorism, and other threats to its security." U.S. Department of Defense, Joint Publication 1-02: *Dictionary of Military and Associated Terms*, March 15, 2013, 145.

[39] U.S. Air Force, *U.S. Air Force Irregular Warfare Tiger Team Observations and Recommendations*, May 22, 2009, 3.

- **Building partner capacity has not traditionally been a designed operational capability requirement, even for units regularly involved with PNs.** Although some new initiatives are coming on-line purely dedicated to building partner capacity, these are more the exception than the rule. In turn, this signals that the majority of USAF individuals, units, and commanders are neither required to maintain training for nor given credit for supporting such activities.

- **The USAF's force providers and personnel system are not optimized for, nor have sufficient personnel needed by, the geographic CCDRs to conduct effective IW.** The USAF's personnel system does not:
    - Track IW related skills;
    - Provide enough manpower at planning staffs to conduct IW;
    - Enable long-term focus and rotations;
    - Provide the most qualified individuals for IW given current military career progression and education requirements;
    - Reward IW skills and assignments;
    - Provide a comprehensive joint information operations and/or IW career progression model; or
    - Assess, select, and train adequate numbers of personnel dedicated to IW, especially in aviation FID.

- **The USAF lacks adequate IW training and education,** especially in:
    - Relevant language, region, and culture skills;
    - Effectively providing IW expertise on component staffs and for advising foreign militaries;
    - Conducting information operations;
    - Planning experience regarding strategic (as opposed to operational) effects;
    - Interacting with other government and non-government organizations; and
    - Informing key decision makers and planners about available IW capabilities.

- **The organizational structures of special operations forces, GPF, and other government agencies limit planning integration and synchronization across the whole-of-government and enduring distributed operations.** For example, only two dedicated GPF advising squadrons currently exist. However, these squadrons, due to the lack of a more appropriate organizational structure, fall within a contingency response wing, whose primary mission is to react to crises, rather than work to prevent and deter conflict. In addition, these squadrons are focused only on air mobility systems, rather than AED as a whole.